The Grab Bag

by Sheldon Kramer
illustrated by Diane Greenseid

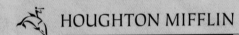

HOUGHTON MIFFLIN   BOSTON

Printed in China

ISBN 10: 0-618-88683-4
ISBN 13: 978-0-618-88683-8

15 16 17 18 19 0940 21 20 19 18 17
4500648152

It was Rosa's birthday. "It is time for the grab
bag," she said. "There are five whistles, three
yo-yos, two cars, and a dog. There is something
for everyone."

The children made a chart to show what was in the bag. "It's Sally's turn to pick a toy," said Ted.

Read • Think • Write   Is Sally more likely to grab the dog or a whistle?

Sally grabbed a whistle! Sue crossed off one whistle on the chart. Now there were only 4 whistles left in the bag. It was Ted's turn.

Read • Think • Write Is Ted less likely to grab a yo-yo or a car?

Ted grabbed the yo-yo! Sally crossed out one yo-yo on the chart. "It's Rosa's turn," said Ted.

Read•Think•Write Do you think Rosa will be more likely to grab a whistle or a car?

Rosa grabbed a whistle! Pablo crossed out one more whistle on the chart. "I wonder what Sue will grab," said Ted.

Read • Think • Write   Is Sue less likely to grab a yo-yo or a car?

6

Sue grabbed another whistle. At last, it was Pablo's turn. What was he likely to grab? Pablo did not grab a car. He did not grab a yo-yo, and he did not grab a whistle. Pablo grabbed the best prize of all. Pablo grabbed the dog!

Toys for All

Show

Predict Outcomes Look at page 5. Draw the toy that Rosa is most likely to grab.

Share

Talk about the chart on page 5. Tell the number of toys it shows.

Write

Look at page 7. Write about the boy who grabbed the dog.